My Very Exciting, Sorta Scary, Big Move

A Workbook for Children Moving to a New Home

Written by
Lori Attanasio Woodring, Ph.D.

Designed by Bobbie Miltcheva

Illustrated by Timm Joy
And you!

My Very Exciting, Sorta Scary, Big Move

A Workbook for Children Moving to a New Home

Recommended for children ages 5-11

First Published in 2013 by Child's View Press

ISBN-13: 978-0615879420
ISBN-10: 061587942X

This book is dedicated to my parents, who taught me the meaning of a loving home, to my husband, whose 12 childhood moves helped to make him the incredible man he is today, and to my four amazing children, who inspired me to write this book.

Table of Contents

Introduction

Moving is among life's biggest stressors. While relocating is extremely hectic and disruptive for parents, it also is quite stressful for kids. Children thrive on familiarity and routine and moving to a new home, no matter how near or far, can be very unsettling. This book will guide you and your child through the experience and help your child make sense of the move in a safe environment. Through drawing and activities, kids will have the opportunity to take control of their feelings and experiences and become active participants in this new adventure.

In this book you will find tools to help your child process the experience of moving, discover meaningful ways to say goodbye and stay in touch, get involved in the process of moving, be proactive in learning about his/her new school and neighborhood, and think about ways to make new friends. This book will expose your child to various strategies to manage emotions; your child will need your help learning and practicing these strategies.

Most parents do their best to shield children from the stressors associated with moving and to focus only on the positive aspects. Yet, children of all ages are capable of having mixed emotions and even strong feelings about moving. They may not choose to share these emotions if they feel they aren't supposed to, but unexpressed feelings can lead to unwanted behaviors, e.g. acting out or withdrawal. It is important to validate your child's feelings and be open to his/her ideas. If you follow through on the strategies your child identifies as helpful throughout this book, it will ease his/her transition and ultimately yours.

You may be hesitant to acknowledge all different feelings as you may fear that your child will become more upset. On the contrary, it is important to help children identify their feelings so they are able manage them. It is not uncommon for children to feel sad, worried, or angry about an upcoming move. If your child isn't feeling these emotions, then asking him/her won't create those feelings. Perhaps he/she will feel that way at some point in the future and by completing the workbook and talking about ways to manage emotions, you will have provided him/her with necessary tools. Teaching children to identify and cope with emotions is an invaluable life skill.

The intention of this workbook is for a child and parent to work together to generate discussions. If your child prefers to work alone, please be sure to review his/her work and ask/answer questions. The exercises are meant to stimulate honest and meaningful conversations in a positive and solution-oriented framework. Most importantly, though, it is my hope that this book enables you and your child to enjoy this exciting new chapter.

A MESSAGE FOR KIDS:

This is a workbook just for you. You can ask a parent to help, or work on it by yourself. Either way, make sure to share your thoughts and ideas with your parents so they know how you are feeling and how they can help you.

Moving is a big change and you may have lots of different feelings or maybe you aren't sure how you feel. This workbook will help you understand and plan for your move. It is packed with activities and ideas to make moving easier and strategies to help you manage your feelings. The strategies you learn can be used any time — not just when you are moving!

Remember, moving is a new adventure with many exciting possibilities. You can keep all of your old friends and make new ones too! There are lots of ways for you to "help" with the move and find out about your new neighborhood and school. This workbook will show you how.

Throughout the book you will be asked to draw or write about your feelings, thoughts, and ideas. Remember, there is NO RIGHT OR WRONG way to do this. This book is all yours, so have fun!

Ready? Set? Let's go...

1 ME AND MY FAMILY

This book belongs to ✏️

....

This is a picture of me. I am .... years old. 🖍️

This is my family.

There are .... people in my family.

I have .... brothers.

I have .... sisters.

I have a pet .... named ....

2 UNDERSTANDING CHANGE

All things change. Change is everywhere.

The seasons change. In spring, the flowers bloom. Some days the sun shines and sometimes it rains. In autumn, the leaves come off the trees. In winter, snow falls from the sky.

Change is exciting.

People change too. You started as a little baby. You grew bigger and learned to talk and walk. You may have even learned to ride a bike. Your hair grew and you got a haircut. You have probably lost your first tooth.

You will continue to grow and change every day and every year.

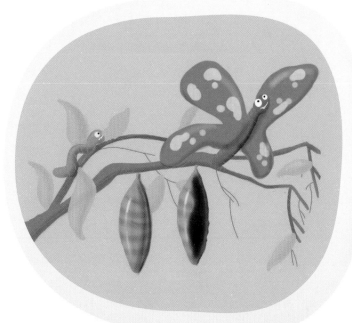

ALL THINGS CHANGE.
CHANGE IS
A PART OF LIFE.

When people *move* they change where they live.

More than 40 million Americans move each year. That is A LOT of people. You are not alone.

Over 6 million Americans have moved abroad, or out of the country they live in, to live in another part of the world.

People move for many different reasons. One reason is for Mom or Dad to take a new job or be closer to the job they have.

Sometimes people move because of a change in their family like divorce, marriage, or a new baby. Sometimes families need a bigger or smaller house.

Other people move to a warmer place or to be closer to family and loved ones.

No matter why people move, moving means a change for the entire family.

Moving can be an exciting adventure but sometimes you might feel scared or worried because you don't know what your new home will be like.

What is the difference between a house and a home?

House

Home

"Home is where my family is..."

⭐ Some of my friends have lived in the same house since they were born.

⭐ Some of my friends have moved one time or many times in their lives.

I have ✏️

☐ never moved   ☐ moved two times
☐ moved once   ☐ moved lots of times

Right now I live in

☐ an apartment   ☐ a house   ☐ a flat
☐ a condominium   ☐ other

This is a picture of where I live. 🖍️CRAYON

My address is .... ✏️

These are my favorite things about where I live.
Circle as many as you like or add your own!

friend

cousin

aunt

neighbor

teacher

grandma

uncle

grandpa

Each new place is different and special. You will be able to do some of your favorite things in your new home and neighborhood too. You will most likely find new favorite things to do. And wherever you move you will make new friends.

My new home will be

☐ an apartment ☐ a house ☐ a flat
☐ a condominium ☐ a castle ☐ other/not sure yet

This is what my new home or town will look like.

My new address will be ....

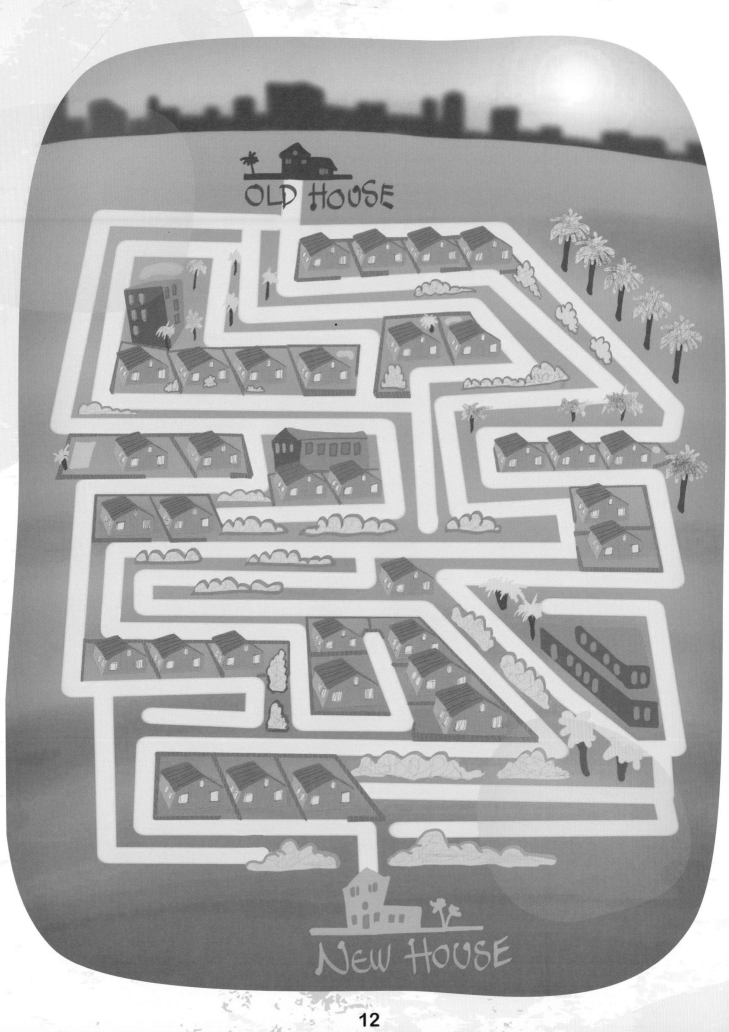

This is what my room looks like now.

This is what I would like my new room to look like.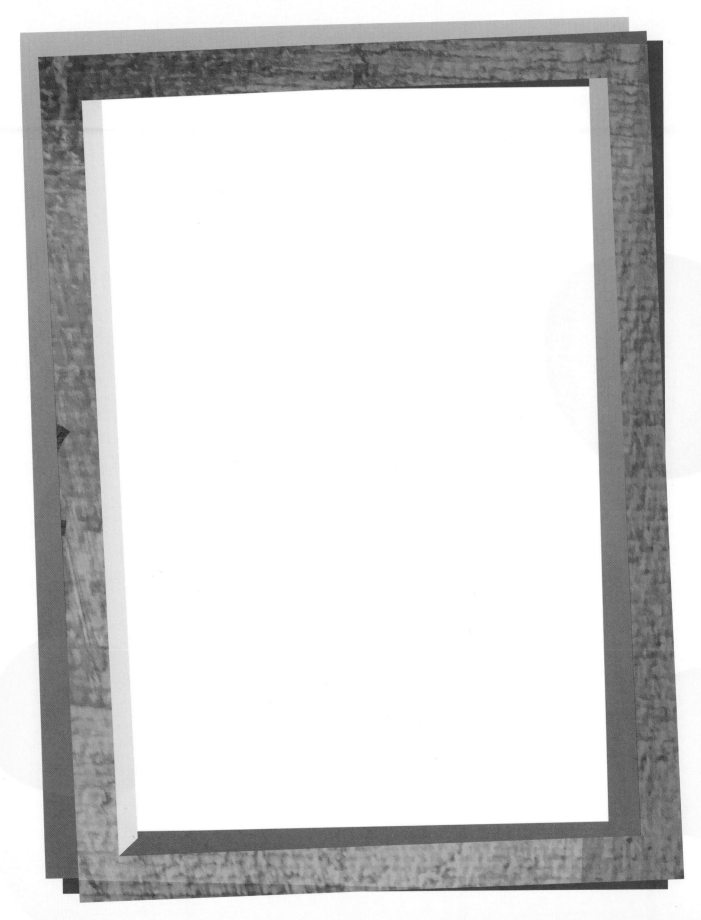

What are the differences between your room now and what your new room will look like? ✏️

....

....

....

Can you make your room look the same or almost the same? ✏️

....

....

....

What changes would you like to make to your new room? ✏️

....

....

....

3 FEELINGS ABOUT MOVING

It is possible to have all kinds of feelings about moving. You can be sad and happy or worried and excited all at the same time. This is normal. All feelings are okay.

*Put a check next to the feelings you have about moving. Underline those feelings that are the strongest. Circle any words you don't know and ask a grown up what they mean.

☐ Excited	☐ Surprised	☐ Eager
☐ Unsure	☐ Frustrated	☐ Brave
☐ Scared	☐ Glad	☐ Mad
☐ Nervous	☐ Alone	☐ Afraid
☐ Worried	☐ Ignored	☐ Loved
☐ Enthusiastic	☐ Confused	☐ Disappointed
☐ Upset	☐ Sad	☐ Special
☐ Happy	☐ Adventurous	☐ Stressed

People can feel all different kinds of feelings. Feelings come from inside our body.

Use the color chart to color the person below and show the places where you feel each feeling.

Happy = Yellow

Mad or Angry = Red

Sad = Blue

Scared = Black

Worried or Nervous = Orange

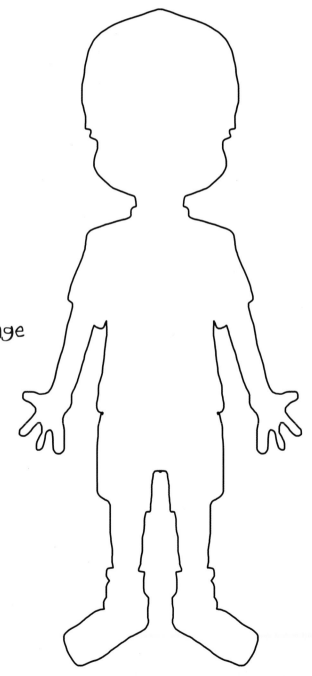

There are both sad and happy things about moving.
Make a list of the sad things and happy things about your move.

* Remember, moving is an opportunity for a new start!

SAD THINGS

(examples)

Will miss seeing my neighbors every day

Will miss my old house

1. ....

2. ....

3. ....

4. ....

5. ....

HAPPY THINGS

(examples)

Will have a nice back yard

Can walk to school

1. ....

2. ....

3. ....

4. ....

5. ....

Write the name of, or draw a face of, the feelings you have about moving and tell why.

I feel   excited   because we are moving to a new house.

I feel   worried   because I need to change schools.

I feel ....   because ....

I feel ....   because ....

I feel ....   because ....

* Now see if you can use an "I feel" statement to tell a grown up how you feel.

4 WHEN YOU'RE SAD

When people move they need to say goodbye. It can be sad to say goodbye. Draw a picture of what you look like when you feel sad.

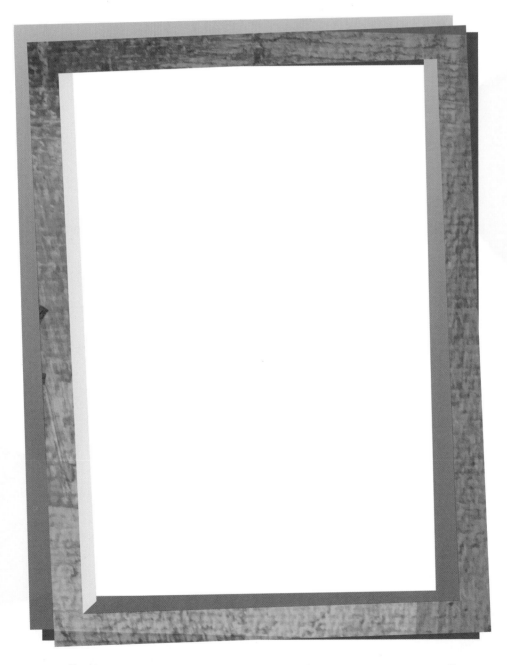

It is okay to feel sad and to cry. Crying helps people feel better.

Draw or write what you do when you feel sad.

Here are some <u>strategies</u>, or things you can do when you feel sad. . .

1. Talk to your mom, dad, or another grown up.
2. Write in a journal.
3. Draw a picture.
4. Go for a walk, bike ride, or scooter ride.
5. Listen to music.
6. Read a book.
7. Play a game.
8. Do a puzzle.
9. Think of a joke.
10. Hug your stuffed animal.
11. Think of what has gone right today.
12. Do a craft project or create something.
13. Go on a swing or rock in a rocking chair.
14. Lie in bed, relax, and take deep belly breaths.

DEEP BELLY BREATHS...

are a great way to relax or feel calm when you are upset, angry, or worried. You can do them anywhere and at any time and no one even needs to know. That's what makes them the best secret strategy!

How to do them:

1. Lie on your back. Close your eyes. Put your hands on your belly.
2. Close your mouth and breathe in through your nose while slowly counting to 5.
   * Pretend you are blowing up a balloon in your belly so your belly grows big when you breathe in.
3. Hold your breath for 3 seconds and then slowly breathe out through your mouth.
   * Pretend you are emptying the big balloon.
4. Now repeat it 5 times or until you feel calm. It will take some practice at first but once you get the hang of it you will be able to do it anywhere... anytime. No need to lie down!

Why they work:

When you are sad or upset your breathing can get faster and you may feel tight in your face and body. Deep belly breaths relax your body and take your mind off of what is upsetting you.

My "Sad Strategy Sack"

Write the 3 strategies you will try the next time you are feeling sad about your move.

1. . . . .
2. . . . .
3. . . . .

You can also write your favorite strategies on pieces of paper and put them into a bag. The next time you feel sad, pull out a piece of paper and you're on your way to feeling better!

5 WHEN YOU'RE MAD

You may also feel mad or angry that you need to move to a new place. **Draw a picture of what you look like when you feel mad.**

It is okay to feel angry. It's what you do with your anger that matters. It isn't okay to hurt someone or something.

Draw or write what you do when you feel angry.

Sometimes when you feel really angry in your whole body you might need to do something active to feel better.

1. Get outside and do something (bike, jump rope, rollerblade, pogo stick, play football, basketball, or baseball, etc.).

2. Go for a walk or run.

3. Do jumping jacks or push-ups.

4. Stomp on an empty box.

5. Sing or dance.

6. Punch your pillow.

Some other things you can do when you feel mad are...

1. Draw an angry picture.

2. Write a note about what is making you mad and crumple it up.

3. Shrink it! Draw a picture of what makes you mad on paper or in your head. Then draw a smaller and smaller and smaller picture of it. Or, imagine the picture getting smaller and smaller and smaller.

4. And don't forget the best secret strategy... deep belly breaths.

My "Mad Strategy Sack"

Write the 3 strategies you will try the next time you are feeling mad about your move.

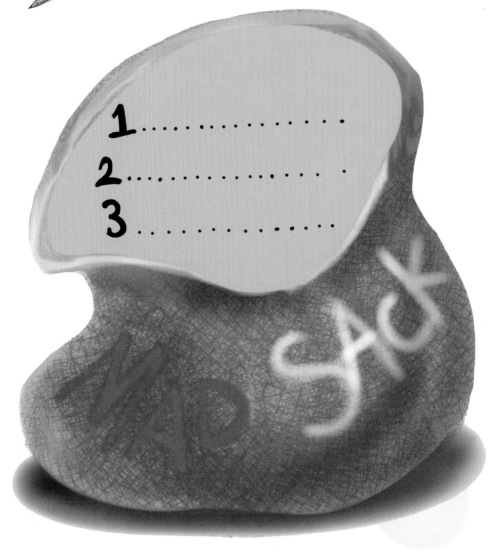

1 . . . .
2 . . . .
3 . . . .

You can also write your favorite strategies on pieces of paper and put them into a bag. The next time you feel mad pull out a piece of paper and you're on your way to feeling better!

6 WHEN YOU'RE WORRIED

A worry is a thought that makes you feel upset. You might feel worry in your body too. Your head may hurt, you might get a strange feeling in your tummy, your hands may sweat, and your heart can beat fast.

Nervous, stressed, and anxious are other words for worried. People sometimes feel this way in new situations — like moving.

Draw a picture of what you look like when you're worried.

Draw or write what you do when you feel worried.

HERE ARE SOME OTHER THINGS YOU CAN DO WHEN YOU WORRY.

1. Lie in bed and concentrate on tightening one part of your body at a time and then relaxing it. First start with your toes, then legs, then tummy, and work your way up to your arms, hands, and face. Tighten and count to 10 and then relax.

2. Exercise (walk, run, bike, or stretch).

3. Listen to music, sing, or dance.

4. Imagine yourself in your favorite place in the world or the place where you feel the most safe, happy, and calm. Think of every detail of your happy place... how it feels and smells... what you see and hear. When you have your place in your mind you can "go" there whenever you are feeling worried.

5. Imagine the funniest story or time that you can think of... and laugh!

6. Give yourself a "Butterfly Hug". Butterfly hugs can calm and relax you. To do them, cross your arms across your chest, as if you were holding yourself, with your right hand resting on your left upper arm and your left hand on your right upper arm. Then, as you think about what is worrying you, tap one hand and then the other, over and over, left, right, left, right. You can do it as fast or slowly as you like. Tap for a while, take a deep breath, and see if you feel better. If not, try again.

7. Take a bath or a shower.

8. Talk to someone.

9. Write in your journal or draw a picture.

10. Make a "worry doll" to tell your worries to so the doll can have the worries and not you! (See page 34.)

11. Write all of your worries on a piece of paper and put it in an envelope. Seal the envelope and decide not to think about the worries until you open it up. Set up a time with a grown up to open the envelope and talk about your worries. Not able to write them down? Just imagine putting each worry, one at a time, in a little box and sealing it up tight.

12. Use calming words. Think of something you can say to yourself over and over to make you feel less worried like: "It's going to be okay." "I know I can do it." "I'm good at making friends." Try to think of a sentence that works for you.

13. And of course. . . take deep belly breaths.

How to Make
a Worry Doll

1. Find a wooden clothespin.

2. Gather some scrap fabric, yarn, string,
   pipe cleaners, sticks, paper, markers, beads,
   stickers, and any other decorations you might want to use.

3. Use the clothespin for the doll's body.

4. Wrap fabric or yarn around the body for clothing.

5. Create arms with pipe cleaners, rolled paper, sticks, or fabric. You
   will need strong glue to glue these so you may need a grown
   up's help.

6. Use some yarn or string for the doll's hair. Glue it on.

7. Make as many as you like.

8. Find a little box to decorate and put your worry dolls in your
   worry box.

9. Finally, whisper your worries to your worry dolls and they will
   hold on to them so you don't have to!

OR. . .

Another simple option is to make "worry stones". Gather some
special rocks or stones from outside, color them or decorate them
if you like, and use them as "worry stones". Find a box or pouch to
keep them in!

My "Worry Strategy Sack"

Write the 3 strategies you will try the next time you are feeling worried about your move.

1 . . . .
2 . . . .
3 . . . .

WORRY SACK

You can also write your favorite strategies on pieces of paper and put them into a bag. The next time you feel worried, pull out a piece of paper and you're on your way to feeling better!

STRATEGY WORD SEARCH

```
c  r  e  a  t  e  d  r  a  w  d  s
z  k  u  j  a  p  i  b  p  c  a  u
m  s  b  k  s  z  o  m  e  q  n  n
i  i  r  e  a  d  s  x  o  v  c  f
m  n  e  j  e  n  t  l  q  g  e  j
a  g  a  e  x  e  r  c  i  s  e  a
g  d  t  t  f  v  a  l  a  u  g  h
i  j  h  a  c  o  t  d  y  t  w  f
n  h  e  l  e  r  e  l  a  x  r  s
e  u  a  k  y  k  g  z  p  y  i  q
y  g  x  c  y  w  y  s  y  a  t  q
c  c  r  p  l  a  y  u  y  s  e  s
```

strategy   hug   relax   breathe   play

exercise   dance   laugh   read   imagine

talk   sing   write   create   draw

CONTRACT

I (name) .... promise that when I am feeling sad, mad, or worried about my move I will use my 3 favorite strategies from my "Strategy Sack" to help me feel better.

Yours Truly,

....

Signature

....

Date

7 SAYING GOODBYE

When you move you may not live close to the same friends and family anymore. You will miss these people but there are so many ways to stay close.

Draw or list the people you want to stay close with after you move.

Draw or list the places you want to remember when you move.

 **IDEA**

Together with your family write a list of all of the people and places you want to visit before you move. Also make a list of all of the places you want to see and explore in your new neighborhood.

These are some ways you can say goodbye to your home and your friends and to prepare for the move. **Put a check next to the ideas you think you will try.**

1. Take photos of your house and room.

2. Take photos of each of your friends.

3. Take photos of your school and favorite places.

4. Have your friends sign a book, pillow case, or t-shirt for you to keep. If you play a sport have them sign a ball, jersey, stick, etc.

5. Make a video of your old house, school, and neighborhood or any of the places you would like to remember.

6. Make a video of each of your friends saying a special goodbye message. Make a video with messages for each of them as well!

7. Make a card or gift for a special friend, teacher, or neighbor. Write down the phone numbers, house addresses, and email addresses of your friends.

8. Make a card with your new address and phone number and give it to your friends.

9. Don't forget to have a goodbye celebration or party. Take photos or videos.

Make a list of your own ideas of how to say goodbye.

1. ....

2. ....

3. ....

4. ....

Make a list of ways you can stay close with your family and friends.

1. ....

2. ....

3. ....

4. ....

Draw a line from each thought to the ideas that might help you feel better and remember your favorite friends and places.

I wish I could see my friends and family.

Draw a picture.
Write a letter.
Write an email.

I'm feeling sad because I miss my old friends.

Send a photo.
Send a text.
Call them on the phone.

I want to remember the special faces, places, and experiences from my old home.

Set up a video call (Skype or Face Time.)
Ask your parents to plan a visit.

I bet my old friends are wondering how I'm doing.

Make a photo album.
Make a scrapbook of notes, photos, and drawings from friends.
Create a memory box.

How to Make a Memory Box

1. Find a box. It can be plastic, cardboard, metal, or wood. A shoe box works well.
2. Decorate the box with markers, paint, stickers, wrapping paper, brown paper you can color, comics, or anything you like.
3. Put your name on the box or label the box with a personal note. You can even write your address.
4. Collect any items you want to save as a memory from your current home.

 **IDEAS**

ticket stubs
a friendship bracelet
cards, letters, or notes
photos of friends
a photo of your house and room
a photo of your favorite place in town
a rock from the garden or shell from the beach
a card from your favorite shop or restaurant
add a small part of something you cannot take along like the bell
from your old bicycle or the sign from your tree house

* add any trinket, treasure, or memory that is special to you and
   reminds you of your old home

8 A NEW ADVENTURE

There are many wonderful and exciting changes that come with moving. Draw or write the most exciting thing about your move.

Even before this move, you probably made other "moves" in your life.

You may have changed schools from your nursery school to a bigger school. Each year you probably moved to a new classroom with a new teacher. Maybe you changed after school activities or moved from one soccer team to another. You might have even changed rooms in your own house!

Moves, transitions, and changes are a **normal** part of life. Each change brings an exciting possibility. Moving is like starting over. It's just like pressing the reset button on a game or getting a "do over". It opens up new possibilities and outcomes.

Can you think of something you might want to "do over" like try out for a team, change your nickname, start a new hobby. . .

I want to. . .

....

....

....

When your family is preparing to move, Mom and Dad might be very busy or stressed about the move too. They will have lots to do. Moving is hard work.

Mom and Dad will feel tired. This doesn't mean they don't have time to talk with you about your feelings. They are working extra hard to make the move go smoothly so it can be easier for you. It may help to get involved in the move.

Draw or write some ways you can get involved in the move.
For example, pick the color of your new room, help clean up and organize your own toys, pack away your special belongings. . .

 **IDEA** Write yourself a note about all the exciting things you want to do in your new home and town. Pack it in one of the boxes and open it when you arrive!

Inside this suitcase draw or write the names of all of the things you would like to take with you to your new home.

The day of the move will be really busy and there will be lots of people and boxes around. It's a good idea to pack your own special box or suitcase to carry with you during the move. You can pack it with your favorite toy, stuffed animal, book, game, or any other thing you might want to have with you at all times.

Draw or list the things you want to take with you on moving day.

You might have lots of questions about the move. Can you write down as many questions as you can think of?

? ....

? ....

? ....

? ....

? ....

? ....

? ....

? ....

Pretend you are a detective and you need to find the answers to all of your questions. **Where will you look? What will you do? How can you find the answers?**

1. ....

2. ....

3. ....

4. ....

5. ....

6. ....

7. ....

8. ....

IDEAS

Ask a parent or relative.

Ask a friend who has moved.

Look for a book or check on the Internet.

* Be sure to ask your mom and dad if the information you got is correct!

9 MY NEW SCHOOL AND NEIGHBORHOOD

The name of my new school is ....

I will be in .... grade.

Can you find out the name of your principal?

Can you find out the names of the teachers in your grade?

The more you can find out about your new school the more comfortable you will be on the first day. Here are some ways you can learn about your school. **Put a check next to the ideas you will try.**

- [ ] 1. Go visit your new school.
- [ ] 2. Set up an appointment with the principal to tour the school.
- [ ] 3. Have your parents take photos of the school building and the classrooms if you can't visit in person.
- [ ] 4. Check the school website for information about the school and teachers.
- [ ] 5. Write a letter to your teacher if you know her name.
- [ ] 6. Call or write to the school and ask for a "Buddy Family" or "Pen Pal" in your grade that you can connect with before moving.
- [ ] 7. See if there are any other new students at the school that you can call.
- [ ] 8. Set up a "play date" or outing with a buddy family or another new student.
- [ ] 9. Ask your parents to contact the Parent Association of the school to find out about ways to join the school community.
- [ ] 10. If you move in the summer attend a local camp to meet neighborhood kids.

My New Neighborhood

I am moving to ....

What I already know about
my new neighborhood...

1. ....

2. ....

3. ....

What I want to know about
my new neighborhood...

1. ....

2. ....

3. ....

How I can find out? **Unscramble the words to get some ideas.**

1. Ask my _ _ _ _ _ _ _ (rapnest).

2. Look on the _ _ _ _ _ _ _ _ (terniten).

3. Check the local _ _ _ _ _ _ _ (bryrali) for books on my new city or town or for travel books (if you are moving to a big city).

4. Contact the Chamber of Commerce for your new _ _ _ _ (ytic) or town and ask for information on things to see and do.

5. Go for a _ _ _ _ _ (sitiv) if possible.

6. See if you can have someone take _ _ _ _ _ _ _ _ _ (citupser) of your new home and neighborhood so you can imagine where you will move.

7. Get a _ _ _ (pam) of your new _ _ _ _ (wotn).

ANSWERS:

1. parents, 2. internet, 3. library, 4. city, 5. visit, 6. pictures, 7. map, town

10 WAYS TO MAKE NEW FRIENDS

1. Walk around the neighborhood with a grown up and introduce yourself to the kids there.

2. Ask for a "buddy family" at school and meet up with them when you move. Maybe they can introduce you to other friends as well.

3. Join a neighborhood or school sports team, the orchestra or band, or chorus.

4. Join school or community clubs such as drama, chess, etc.

5. Invite new friends over for play dates — the best way to make new friends is to spend time together. Your parents can help you organize this.

6. Ask your parents to host a neighborhood "moving in" party.

7. Make some cookies or treats and deliver them to your new neighbors.

8. Get involved in religious or community groups.

9. Have a lemonade stand on your block.

10. Go out of your way to be friendly. Say "hi" to new people and ask them to join in your activities or ask if you could join in with them!

Draw or write about how you met some of your favorite friends.
Can you meet new friends the same way?

Draw a picture of an activity that you would like to do with your new friends.

11 WHAT I KNOW ABOUT MOVING

I now know that...

1. ....

2. ....

3. ....

4. ....

5. ....

6. ....

7. ....

8. ....

True or False

Answer with "T" for true or "F" for false. ✏️

1. .... All things change. Change is a normal part of life.

2. .... Most kids have all sorts of feelings about moving, some good and some bad.

3. .... I should not tell my parents if I feel upset or worried or they might feel bad.

4. .... I should not get angry. It is a bad feeling.

5. .... There is nothing I can do to stop my worrying.

6. .... When I am feeling sad I can draw a picture or write in a journal.

7. .... I can do deep belly breaths anywhere at any time to relax.

8. .... I can only feel worry in my head, not in my whole body.

9. .... "I am good at meeting new people" is an example of using calming words.

10. .... Some fun things to do to say goodbye include making a memory box, taking photos of favorite people and places, and having a goodbye party.

11. .... There are lots of ways I can stay in touch with my friends.

12. .... It is a good idea to pack my own special bag or box on the day of the move to take important things with me.

13. .... If I have any questions at all about moving or my new home or neighborhood I should ask a grown up.

14. .... If I want to learn about my new school I can check the website, call the principal, take a tour, or ask for a "buddy family".

15. .... I will make new friends wherever I go!

ANSWERS:

1. True. 2. True. 3. False. 4. False. 5. False. 6. True. 7. True. 8. False. 9. True. 10. True. 11. True. 12. True. 13. True. 14. True. 15. True.

CERTIFICATE OF COMPLETION

CONGRATULATIONS!

You now understand that all things change and change can be really exciting. You have explored your feelings about moving and learned some important strategies to help you when you feel sad, mad, or worried. You are ready to start a new adventure and have all the tools to make it a successful one!

This award goes to

....
(Name)

For completing this workbook on

....
(Date)

WELL DONE

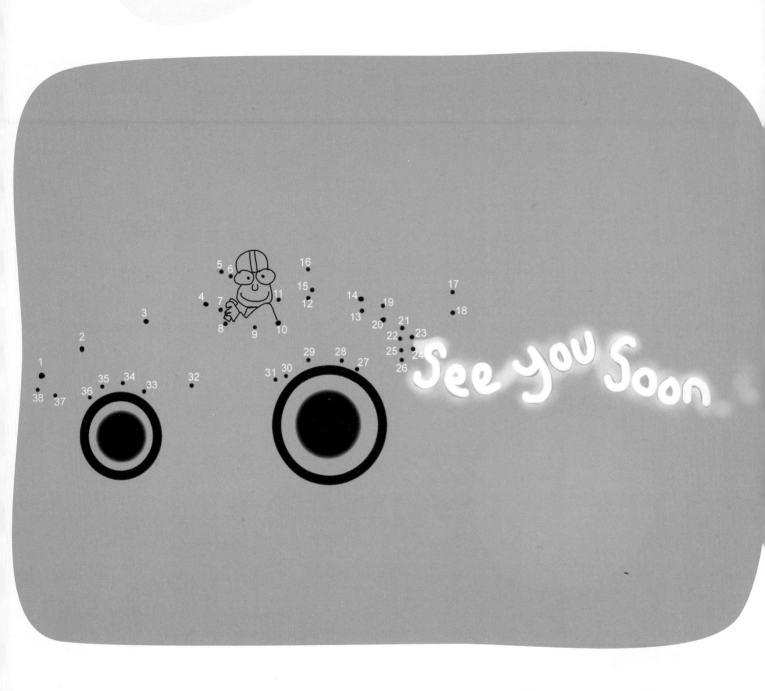

Remember . . . No matter where you live or how different your life may be, you will always be loved by your family!

My Special Thoughts,
Ideas, or Drawings

(Feel free to write or draw about anything at all!)